Dr. Jaerock Lee

Faith:
THE ASSURANCE OF THINGS HOPED FOR

> *"Now faith is the assurance of things hoped for,*
> *the conviction of things not seen.*
> *... And without faith it is impossible to please Him*
> *for he who comes to God must believe that*
> *He is and that He is a rewarder*
> *of those who seek Him."*
> *(Hebrews 11:1, 6)*

FAITH by Dr. Jaerock Lee
Published by Urim Books (Representative: Kyungtae Noh)
73, Yeouidaebang-ro 22-gil, Dongjak-Gu, Seoul, Korea
www.urimbooks.com
Subtitle: The Assurance of Things Hoped for

All rights reserved. This book or parts thereof may not be reproduced in any form, stored in a retrieval system, or transmitted in any form or by any means, electronic, mechanical, photocopying, recording or otherwise, without prior written permission of the publisher.

Unless otherwise noted, all Scripture quotations are taken from the Holy Bible, NEW AMERICAN STANDARD BIBLE,®, Copyright © 1960, 1962, 1963, 1968, 1971, 1972, 1973, 1975, 1977, 1995 by The Lockman Foundation. Used by permission.

Copyright © 2009 by Dr. Jaerock Lee
ISBN: 978-89-7557-229-6, ISBN: 978-89-7557-060-5(set)
Translated by Dr. Esther Kooyoung Chung. Used by permission.

Previously published in Korean by Urim Books, Seoul, Korea.
Copyright © 1990

First Published July 2009

Edited by Dr. GeumSun Vin
Designed by Editorial Bureau
Printed in Seoul, Korea
For more information contact at urimbook@hotmail.com

Prologue

"Now faith is the assurance of things hoped for, the conviction of things not seen. For by it the men of old gained approval. By faith we understand that the worlds were prepared by the word of God, so that what is seen was not made out of things which are visible" (Hebrews 11: 1-3).

Above all else, I give all thanks and glory to God the Father who has led us to publish this book.

God, who is love, sent His only begotten Son, Jesus Christ, as the atoning sacrifice for mankind who were doomed to death because of their sin since the disobedience of Adam and paved the path to salvation for us. With faith in this fact, anyone who opens his heart and accepts Jesus Christ as his Savior is forgiven of his sins, receives the gift of the Holy Spirit and is recognized as a child of God by Him. Moreover, as a child of God he is entitled to receive answers to whatever he asks for by faith. The result of which is the abundant life with no insufficiency, and he will have the ability to triumphantly overcome the world.

The Bible tells us that the fathers of faith believed in the power of God to create something out of nothing. They came to experience the amazing works of God. Our God is the same yesterday, today and tomorrow, and with His almighty power

He is still performing the same works for those who believe and practice the word of God recorded in the Bible.

In my ministry during the past decade, I have witnessed countless Manmin members who have received answers and solutions to various problems they had once suffered in their lives by believing and obeying the word of truth and they were able to greatly give glory to God. When they believed the word of God saying, *"The kingdom of heaven suffers violence, and violent men take it by force"* (Matthew 11:12), and they have toiled and prayed and practiced the word of God in order to possess greater faith, they looked more precious and beautiful to me than anything else.

This work is for those who eagerly wish to lead victorious lives by possessing true faith to glorify God, spreading the love of God and sharing the gospel of the Lord. For the last two decades I have preached so many messages entitled "Faith" and through choosing from among them and editing them in an orderly manner, this book was made possible to be printed. I wish for this work, *Faith: The Assurance of Things Hoped for*, to play the role of a lighthouse that acts as a guide to true faith for countless souls.

The wind blows where it wishes and it is invisible to our eyes. Yet, when we see the trees' leaves swaying in the wind, we can sense the reality of the wind. By the same token, though you are not able to actually see God with the naked eye, God is alive and really exists. That is why in accordance with your faith in Him, to whatever degree you desire, you will be able to see Him, hear Him, sense His presence and experience Him.

Jaerock Lee

Table of Contents

Chapter 1

Fleshly Faith and Spiritual Faith · 1

Chapter 2

The Mind Set on the Flesh Is Hostile toward God · 13

Chapter 3

Destroy All Kinds of Thoughts and Theories · 29

Chapter 4

Sow the Seeds of Faith · 43

Chapter 5

'If You can?' All Things Are Possible! · 57

Chapter 6

Daniel Relied only on God · 71

Chapter 7

God Provides in Advance · 85

Chapter 1

Fleshly Faith and Spiritual Faith

Hebrews 11:1-3

Now faith is the assurance of things hoped for, the conviction of things not seen. For by it the men of old gained approval. By faith we understand that the worlds were prepared by the word of God, so that what is seen was not made out of things which are visible.

A pastor takes delight in seeing his flock possess true faith and glorify God with true faith. On the one hand, when some of them bear witnesses to the living God and testify to their lives in Christ, the pastor can rejoice and become more fervent for his task assigned by God. On the other hand, when some others fail to improve their faith and fall into trials and afflictions, the pastor has to feel the pain and his heart is troubled.

Without faith, it is not only impossible for you to please God and to receive His answers to your prayers, but it would also be very difficult for you to possess the hope for heaven and to lead a proper life of faith.

Faith is the most important foundation in a Christian's life. It is the shortcut to salvation and essentially a necessity in receiving answers of God. In our times, because people have no idea of the right definition of faith, many people fail to possess true faith. They fail to have the assurance of salvation. They fail to walk in the light and fail to receive God's answers even though they confess their faith in God.

Faith is divided into two categories: fleshly faith and spiritual faith. This first chapter explains to you about what the true faith is and how you can receive answers of God and be guided on the path to eternal life through true faith.

Fleshly Faith

When you believe what is seen with your eyes and the things that are agreeable with your knowledge and thoughts, your faith is the type called "fleshly faith." With this fleshly faith you can only believe in those things that are made out of the things that are visible. For example, with this you believe that a desk is made of wood.

Fleshly faith is also called the "faith as knowledge." With this fleshly faith, you believe only what is in agreement with the knowledge stored in your brain and your thoughts. You may believe without doubts that a desk is made of wood because you have seen or heard that a desk is made of wood and have the understanding of it.

People have a memory system in the brain. They input many kinds of knowledge into it from birth. They store into the brain cells the knowledge that they have seen, heard, acquired through their parents, brothers and sisters, friends, and neighbors and are taught at schools, and utilize the stored knowledge as needed.

Not every piece of the knowledge stored in their brain belongs to the truth. The word of God is the truth because it stands forever, while the knowledge from the world easily changes and is the mixture of truth and untruth. Because they do not have the complete understanding of the truth, people of the world do not realize that untruths are being misused as if they were truths. For example, they believe the theory of evolution is right because they have learned only the theory of evolution in school without knowing the word of God.

Those who have been taught only the fact that things are made of something that already exists cannot believe that something is made out of nothingness.

If a man who has fleshly faith is forced to believe something is made of nothingness, the knowledge that he has stored and believed right since his birth prevents him from believing it, and his doubts accompany him and he fails to believe it.

In the third chapter of John, a ruler of the Jews named Nicodemus came to Jesus and shared spiritual talks with Him. During the conversation Jesus challenged him, saying, *"If I told you earthly things and you do not believe, how will you believe if I tell you heavenly things?"* (v. 12)

When you begin your Christian life, you store the knowledge of the word of God as much as you hear it. But you cannot completely believe it from the beginning, and your faith is found to be fleshly. With this fleshly faith, doubts arise within you and you fail to live by the word of God, communicate with God, and to receive His love. That's why fleshly faith is also called the "faith without actions," or "dead faith."

With fleshly faith you cannot be saved. Jesus said in Matthew 7:21, *"Not everyone who says to Me, 'Lord, Lord,' will enter the kingdom of heaven, but he who does the will of My Father who is in heaven will enter"* and in Matthew 3:12, *"His winnowing fork is in His hand, and He will thoroughly clear His threshing floor; and He will gather His wheat into the barn, but He will burn up the chaff with unquenchable fire."* In short, if you do not practice the word of God and your faith turns out to be the faith without deeds, you cannot enter the kingdom of heaven.

Spiritual Faith

When you believe in the things that cannot be seen and things that do not agree with human thoughts and knowledge, you can be deemed to have spiritual faith. With this spiritual faith you can believe that something is made out of nothingness.

Regarding spiritual faith, Hebrews 11:1 defines it as the following: *"Now faith is the assurance of things hoped for, the conviction of things not seen."* In other words, when you look at the things with the spiritual eyes, the things will become reality to you and when you see with the eyes of faith what is not seen, the conviction by which you can believe is revealed. In spiritual faith what cannot be done with fleshly faith, which is faith known as "the faith as knowledge," will be made possible and revealed as a reality.

For example, when Moses saw the things with the eyes of faith, the Red Sea was parted into two and the people of Israel crossed it on the dry land (Exodus 14:21-22). And when Joshua, the successor to Moses, and his people looked at the city of Jericho and marched around the city for 7 days and then shouted at the city wall, the city fell down (Joshua 6:12-20). Abraham, the father of faith, could obey the command of God and offer his only son, Isaac, who was the seed of the promise of God because he believed that God would be able to raise a man from the dead (Genesis 22:3-12). This is one reason why spiritual faith is called the "faith accompanied with actions," and "living faith."

Hebrews 11:3 says, *"By faith we understand that the worlds were prepared by the word of God, so that what is seen was not made out of things which are visible."* The heavens and the earth and all things in them including the sun, the moon, stars, trees, birds, fish, and beasts, were created by the word of God and He formed mankind from the ground. All these were made out of nothingness, and we can believe and understand this fact only by spiritual faith.

Not everything was seen to our eyes or visible reality, but by the power of God, that is, by His word, everything was made. That's why we confess that God is almighty and all-knowing, and from Him we can receive anything that we have asked by faith. It is because the almighty God is our Father and we are His children, so everything is done for us as we have believed.

In order to receive answers and experience miracles by faith, you have to turn your fleshly faith into the faith that is spiritual. First of all, you have to understand that the knowledge stored in the brain since your birth and fleshly faith formed based on that knowledge prevent you from possessing spiritual faith. You have to demolish the knowledge that brings doubts, and remove the knowledge that has been misleadingly stored in your brain. As much as you listen to and understand the word of God, the knowledge of spirit is increasingly stored within you and to the extent that you witness signs and wonders revealed by the power of God and experience the evidences of the living God manifested through many believers' testimonies, doubts are cast away and your spiritual faith grows.

As much as your spiritual faith grows, you can live by the word of God, have the communication with Him, and receive answers from Him. When your doubts are completely cast away, you can stand on the rock of faith and be deemed to posses the strong faith by which you can lead a victorious life in any trial and test.

With this rock of faith, James 1:6 warns us, *"But he must ask in faith without any doubting, for the one who doubts is like the surf of the sea, driven and tossed by the wind,"* and James 2:14 asks us, *"What use is it, my brethren, if someone says he has faith but he has no works? Can that faith save him?"*

Therefore, I urge you to remember that only when you cast away all doubts, stand on the rock of faith and show the deeds of faith, can you be deemed to possess spiritual and true faith by which you can be saved.

True Faith and Eternal Life

The parable of ten virgins recorded in the twenty-fifth chapter of Matthew gives us many teachings. The parable says that ten virgins took their lamps and went out to meet the bridegroom. Five of them were prudent and took oil in flasks along with their lamps and successfully received the bridegroom, but since the other five were foolish and took no oil along with their lamps, they could not meet the bridegroom. This parable explains to us that among the believers some who lead faithful believing lives and are preparing for the return of the Lord with spiritual faith will be saved, while others who do not properly prepare will not be able to gain salvation because their faith is dead faith that is not accompanied with actions.

Through Matthew 7:22-23, Jesus awakens us that even though many have prophesied, cast out demons and performed miracles in His name, not every of them can be saved. It is because they turn out to be the chaff that have not done the will of God but instead practiced lawlessness and committed sins.

How can we discern between the wheat and the chaff?

The Compact Oxford English Dictionary refers to 'chaff' as 'the husks of grain or other seed separately winnowing or threshing.' The chaff spiritually symbolizes the believers who seem to live by the word of God but commit evils without changing their hearts by the truth. They go to church every Sunday, give their tithes, pray to God, take care of weak members and serve the church, but they do all those things, not before God, but to make a show before the eyes of the people around them. That's why they are categorized as the chaff and cannot receive salvation.

The wheat refers to the believers who have turned into men of spirit by the word of truth of God and possess the faith which is not shaken in any circumstances and does not turn to the left or to the right. They do everything by faith: They fast by faith and pray to God by faith, so that they can receive answers from God. They do not act by the force exerted by others, but do everything with joy and thanksgiving. Since they follow the voice of the Holy Spirit to please God and act by faith, their souls prosper, everything goes well with them and they enjoy good health.

Now I urge you to examine yourself whether you have worshiped God in truth and spirit or drowsed and followed idle thoughts and judged the word of God during the worship services. You must also look back and see whether you have given the offerings joyfully or sowed only sparingly or unwillingly because of the eyes of others. The stronger your spiritual faith grows, the more the deeds will follow you. And as much as you practice the word of God, living faith is given to you, and you dwell in the love and blessing of God, walk with Him, and are successful in everything. All the blessings recorded in the Bible will come upon you because God is faithful to His promises just as written in Numbers 23:19, *"God is not a man, that He should lie, nor a son of man, that He should repent; has He said, and will He not do it? Or has He spoken, and will He not make it good?"*

However, if you have attended the worship services and prayed on a regular basis and served the church diligently but fail to receive the desires of the heart, then you have to understand that there is something wrong on your part.

If you have true faith, you have to follow and practice the word of God. Instead of insisting on your own thoughts and knowledge, you should acknowledge that only the word of God is the truth and take courage in destroying whatever is against the word of God. You have to throw away every form evil by means of diligently listening to the word of God and accomplish sanctification through unceasing prayers.

It is not true that you are saved through simply attending the church services and through hearing the word of God and storing it as knowledge. Unless you practice it, it is dead faith without deeds. Only when you possess true and spiritual faith and do the will of God, will you be able to enter the kingdom of heaven and enjoy eternal life.

May you realize that God wants you to have spiritual faith that is accompanied with the actions, and enjoy eternal life and the privilege of the children of God with true faith!

Chapter 2

The Mind Set on the Flesh Is Hostile toward God

Romans 8:5-8

For those who are according to the flesh set their minds on the things of the flesh, but those who are according to the Spirit, the things of the Spirit. For the mind set on the flesh is death, but the mind set on the Spirit is life and peace, because the mind set on the flesh is hostile toward God; for it does not subject itself to the law of God, for it is not even able to do so and those who are in the flesh cannot please God.

Today there are so many people who attend church and profess their faith in Jesus Christ. This is happy and good news to us. But our Lord Jesus said in Matthew 7:21, *"Not everyone who says to Me, 'Lord, Lord,' will enter the kingdom of heaven, but he who does the will of My Father who is in heaven will enter."* And He added in Matthew 7:22-23, *"Many will say to Me on that day, 'Lord, Lord, did we not prophesy in Your name, and in Your name cast out demons, and in Your name perform many miracles?' And then I will declare to them, 'I never knew you; depart from Me, you who practice lawlessness.'"*

And James 2:26 tells us, *"For just as the body without the spirit is dead, so also faith without works is dead."* That's why you have to make your faith complete through deeds of obedience so that you can be recognized as true children of God who receive anything that you have asked for.

After we accept Jesus Christ as our Savior, we come to delight in and serve the law of God with our mind. However, if we fail to keep the commands of God, then we serve the law of sin with our flesh and we fail to please Him. It is because with fleshly thoughts we are put into a position of hostility toward God and are not able to become subject to the law of God.

But if we cast off fleshly thoughts and follow spiritual thoughts, we can be led by the Spirit of God, keep His commands and please Him just the way Jesus fulfilled the law with love. Thus, the promise of God saying, "All things are possible to him who believes," comes upon us.

Now let's delve into what the difference between fleshly and spiritual thoughts is. Let's see why the fleshly thoughts are hostile against God, and how we can avoid fleshly thoughts and walk according to the Spirit so as to please God.

A Fleshly Man Thinks of Fleshly Desires, while a Spiritual Man Desires Things of the Spirit

1) The Flesh and the Desires of the Flesh

In the Bible we find such terminology as 'the flesh,' 'things of the flesh,' 'desires of the flesh,' and 'works of the flesh.' These words are similar in meaning, and all become decayed and disappear after we leave this world.

The **deeds/works of the flesh** are recorded in Galatians 5:19-21: *"Now the deeds of the flesh are evident, which are: immorality, impurity, sensuality, idolatry, sorcery, enmities, strife, jealousy, outbursts of anger, disputes, dissensions, factions, envying, drunkenness, carousing, and things like these, of which I forewarn you, just as I have forewarned you, that those who practice such things will not inherit the kingdom of God."*

In Romans 13:12-14, the apostle Paul warns us of the **desires of the flesh**, saying, *"The night is almost gone, and the* *day is near. Therefore let us lay aside the deeds of darkness and put on the armor of light. Let us behave properly as in the day, not in carousing and drunkenness, not in sexual promiscuity and sensuality, not in strife and jealousy. But put on the Lord Jesus Christ, and make no provision for the flesh in regard to its lusts."*

We have a mind and we have thoughts. When we harbor sinful desires and untruths in our minds, those sinful desires and untruths are called the "desires of the flesh," and when those sinful desires are revealed as actions, they are called the "deeds of the flesh." The desires and the deeds of the flesh are against the truth, so no one who indulges in them can inherit the kingdom of God.

Therefore, God warns us in 1 Corinthians 6:9-10, *"Or do you not know that the unrighteous will not inherit the kingdom of God? Do not be deceived; neither fornicators, nor idolaters, nor adulterers, nor effeminate, nor homosexuals, nor thieves, nor the covetous, nor drunkards, nor revilers, nor swindlers, will inherit the kingdom of God,"* and also in 1 Corinthians 3:16-17, *"Do you not know that you are a temple of God and that the Spirit of God dwells in you? If any man destroys the temple of God, God will destroy him, for the temple of God is holy, and that is what you are."*

As said in the above passages, you have to realize that the unrighteous who commit sins and evils in actions cannot inherit the kingdom of God – those who practice the deeds of the flesh cannot be saved. Stay awake in order not to fall into temptation of the preachers who say that we can be saved by just attending church. In the name of the Lord I implore that you must not fall into the temptation by carefully examining the word of God.

2) The Spirit and Desires of the Spirit

A man consists of spirit, soul and body; our body is perishing. The body only houses our spirit and soul. The spirit and soul are imperishable entities that take charge of the operation of our mind and endow us with life.

The spirit is classified into two categories: The spirit that belongs to God and the spirit that does not belong to God. That's why 1 John 4:1 says, *"Beloved, do not believe every spirit, but test the spirits to see whether they are from God, because many false prophets have gone out into the world."*

The Spirit of God helps us confess that Jesus Christ has come in the flesh, and leads us to know the things freely given to us by God (1 John 4:2; 1 Corinthians 2:12).

Jesus said in John 3:6, *"That which is born of the flesh is flesh, and that which is born of the Spirit is spirit."* If we accept Jesus Christ and receive the Holy Spirit, the Holy Spirit comes into our hearts, strengthens us to understand the word of God, helps us to live according to the word of truth, and leads us to become men of spirit. When the Holy Spirit comes into our heart, He makes our dead spirits alive again, so it is said that we are born again of the Spirit and become sanctified through the circumcision of heart.

Our Lord Jesus said in John 4:24, *"God is spirit, and those who worship Him must worship in spirit and truth."* Spirit belongs to the fourth dimensional world, and so God who is spirit not only sees the heart of each of us but also knows everything about us.

In John 6:63, saying that *"It is the Spirit who gives life; the flesh profits nothing; the words that I have spoken to you are spirit and are life,"* Jesus explains to us that the Holy Spirit gives us life and the word of God is spirit.

And John 14:16-17 say, *"I will ask the Father, and He will give you another Helper, that He may be with you forever; that is the Spirit of truth, whom the world cannot receive, because it does not see Him or know Him, but you know Him because He abides with you and will be in you."* If we receive the Holy Spirit and become the children of God, the Holy Spirit leads us to the truth.

The Holy Spirit dwells within us after we accept the Lord, gives birth to spirit in us, and leads us to the truth. He helps us realize all unrighteousness, and repent of and turn away from them. If we walk against the truth, the Holy Spirit groans, makes us feel troubled, encourages us to realize our sins and accomplish sanctification.

In addition, the Holy Spirit is called the Spirit of God (1 Corinthians 12:3) and the Spirit of the Lord (Acts 5:9; 8:39). The Spirit of God is the everlasting Truth and the life-giving Spirit and leads us to eternal life.

On the other hand, the spirit which does not belong to God but is against the Spirit of God does not confess that Jesus came into this world in flesh, and is called the 'spirit of the world' (1 Corinthians 2:12), the 'spirit of antichrist' (1 John 4:3), 'deceitful spirits' (1 Timothy 4:1), and 'unclean spirits' (Revelation 16:13). All these spirits are from the devil. They are not from the Spirit of truth. These spirits of untruths do not give life but instead drive people into destruction.

The Holy Spirit refers to the perfect Spirit of God, and thus when we accept Jesus Christ and become God's children, we receive the Holy Spirit, and the Holy Spirit gives birth to spirit and righteousness in us, and strengthens us to bear the fruit of the Holy Spirit, righteousness and the Light. As we resemble God through this work of the Holy Spirit, we will be led by Him, be called sons of God, and call God "Abba! Father!" because we receive a spirit of adoption as sons (Romans 8:12-15).

Therefore, as much as we are led by the Holy Spirit, we bear the nine fruits of the Holy Spirit that are love, joy, peace, patience, kindness, goodness, faithfulness, gentleness, and self-control (Galatians 5:22-23). We also bear the fruit of righteousness, and the fruits of the Light that consist in all goodness and righteousness and truth, with which we can reach full salvation (Ephesians 5:9).

Fleshly Thoughts Lead to Death, but Spiritual Thoughts Lead to Life and Peace

If you follow the flesh, you come to set your mind on the things of the flesh. You will live according to the flesh, and commit sins. Then, according to the word of God saying that "The wages of sins is death," you cannot but be led to death. That's why the Lord asks us, *"What use is it, my brethren, if someone says he has faith but he has no works? Can that faith save him? Even so faith, if it has no works, is dead, being by itself"* (James 2:14, 17).

If you set your mind on the flesh, it does not only cause you to sin and to suffer troubles on the earth, but you will not be able to inherit the kingdom of heaven. So, you have to bear this in mind and put the deeds of body to death so that you can gain eternal life (Romans 8:13).

On the contrary, if you follow the Spirit, you come to set

your mind on the Spirit and try your best to live by the truth. Then the Holy Spirit will help you fight against the enemy devil and Satan, cast off untruths and walk in the truth, and then you become sanctified.

Suppose someone strikes you on the cheek without reason. You may feel enraged, but you can drive out fleshly thoughts and follow spiritual ones instead by remembering the crucifixion of Jesus. Because the word of God tells us to turn to him the other cheek when we are struck on one cheek and to rejoice always in any circumstances, you can forgive, patiently endure, and serve the other. As a result, you don't have to be troubled. In this way you can gain peace in your heart. Until you become sanctified, you may want to reproach and rebuke him because evil remains within you. But, after you have cast off every form of evil, you feel love toward him even though you find his faults.

Thus, if you set your mind on the spirit, you seek for spiritual things and walk in the word of truth. Then as a result you can gain salvation and true life, and your life will be filled with peace and blessing.

Fleshly Thoughts Are Hostile Toward God

Fleshly thoughts hinder you from praying to God, while spiritual ones urge you to pray to Him. Fleshly thoughts result in enmity and quarrels, while spiritual ones lead to love and peace. Likewise, fleshly thoughts are against the truth, and they are actually the will and thoughts from the enemy devil. That's why if you continue to follow fleshly thoughts, the barrier will be built up against God, and it will get in the way of God's will for you.

Fleshly thoughts bring no peace but only worries, anxieties, and troubles. In a word, fleshly thoughts are completely meaningless and benefit nothing. Our Father God is almighty and all-knowing, and as the Creator is ruling over the heavens and the earth and all things in them, and also our spirits and bodies. What couldn't He give us His beloved children? If your father is the president of a great industrial group, you would never have to worry about money, and if your father is a perfect medical doctor, good health is guaranteed for you.

As Jesus said in Mark 9:23, *"'If You can?' All things are possible to him who believes,"* spiritual thoughts bring faith and peace on you, while fleshly thoughts prevent you from accomplishing the will and works of God by giving you worries, anxieties and troubles. That's why, regarding fleshly thoughts, Romans 8:7 says, *"Because the mind set on the flesh is hostile toward God; for it does not subject itself to the law of God, for it is not even able to do so."*

We are the children of God who serve God and call Him "Father." If you have no joy but feel troubled, disheartened, and worried instead, however, it proves that you follow fleshly thoughts triggered by the enemy devil and Satan instead of spiritual thoughts that are given by God. Then, you have to repent of it immediately, turn away from it, and seek spiritual thoughts. It is because we can submit ourselves to God and obey Him only with spiritual minds.

Those Who Are in the Flesh Cannot Please God

Those who set their minds on the flesh are found to be against God and do not and cannot submit to the law of God. They disobey God and cannot please Him, and finally suffer from trials and troubles.

Since Abraham, the father of faith, always sought spiritual thoughts, he could obey even the command of God requiring that his only son Isaac be offered as a burnt offering. On the contrary, King Saul, who followed fleshly thoughts, was finally forsaken; Jonah was tossed by a strong storm and swallowed by a great fish; The Israelites had to suffer the forty years of tough life in wilderness after the Exodus.

When you follow spiritual thoughts and show the deeds of faith, you can be given the desires of your hearts, just as promised in Psalm 37:4-6, *"Delight yourself in the LORD; and He will give you the desires of your heart. Commit your way to the LORD, trust also in Him, and He will do it. He will bring forth your righteousness as the light and your judgment as the noonday."*

Anyone who really believes God has to drive out all disobediences caused by the works of the enemy devil, keep the commands of God, and do the things that are pleasing to Him. Then he will become a man of spirit who will be able to receive whatever he has asked for.

How Can We Follow Works of the Spirit?

Jesus, who is the Son of God, came to this earth and became a grain of wheat for sinners and died for them. He paved the path to salvation for anyone who accepts Him to become a child of God, and has reaped countless fruits. He only sought spiritual thoughts and obeyed the will of God; He brought the dead back to life again, healed the sick of all kinds of diseases and expanded the kingdom of God.

What are you to do in order to take after Jesus and to please God?

First of all, you have to live in the help of the Holy Spirit through prayers.

If you do not pray, you will come under the works of Satan and live according to fleshly thoughts. However, when you pray without ceasing, you can receive the works of the Holy

Spirit in your life, be convinced of what is righteous, be in opposition to sin, be free of judgment, follow the desires of the Holy Spirit and be made righteous in the sight of God. Even the Son of God, Jesus, accomplished works of God through prayers. As it is the will of God to pray without ceasing, when you do not cease praying, you can follow only spiritual thoughts and please God.

Secondly, you have to accomplish spiritual works even though you don't want to. The faith without deeds is just the faith as knowledge. It is dead faith. When you know what you have to do, but do not do it, it is sin. So, if you want to follow the will of God and please Him, you have to show the deeds of faith.

Thirdly, you have to repent and receive power from above so that you can possess the faith that is accompanied by actions. Since fleshly thoughts are hostile toward God, displeasing to Him and build up walls of sin between God and you, you have to repent of them and throw them away. Repentance is always needed for a good Christian life, but in order to throw them away you have to rend your heart and repent of them.

If you commit the sins that you know you should not do, your heart feels uncomfortable. When you repent the sins with tearful prayers, worries and anxieties will leave you, you become refreshed, reconciled to God, restored in peace, and you can then receive the desires of your heart. If you continue to pray in order to get rid of every form of evil, you will repent of your sins rending your heart. Your sinful attributes will be burned up by the fire of the Holy Spirit, and the walls of sins be destroyed. Then, you will be able to live by the works of the Spirit and please God accordingly.

If you feel burdened in your heart after you have received the Holy Spirit through faith in Jesus Christ, it is because you have now found yourself to be against God because of your fleshly thoughts. So, you have to destroy the walls of sins through fervent prayers, and then follow the desires of the Holy Spirit and do works of the Spirit according to spiritual thoughts. As a result, peace and joy will come upon your heart, answers to your prayers will be given you and desires of your heart fulfilled.

As Jesus said in Mark 9:23, *"'If You can?' All things are possible to him who believes,"* may each of you throw away fleshly thoughts that are against God and walk by faith according to the works of the Holy Spirit so that you can please God, do His boundless works, and magnify His kingdom, in the name of our Lord Jesus Christ I pray!

Chapter 3

Destroy All Kinds of
Thoughts and Theories

2 Corinthians 10:3-6

For though we walk in the flesh, we do not war according to the flesh, for the weapons of our warfare are not of the flesh, but divinely powerful for the destruction of fortresses. We are destroying speculations and every lofty thing raised up against the knowledge of God, and we are taking every thought captive to the obedience of Christ, and we are ready to punish all disobedience, whenever your obedience is complete..

Again, faith can be divided into two categories: Spiritual faith and fleshly faith. Fleshly faith can also be called the faith that is knowledge. When you first listen to the word of God, you come to have the faith as knowledge. That is fleshly faith. But as much as you understand and practice the word, you come to possess spiritual faith.

If you understand the spiritual meanings of the word of truth of God and lay the foundation of faith by practicing it, God will rejoice and give you spiritual faith. Thus with this spiritual faith given from above, you receive answers to your prayers and solutions to your problems. You will also experience meeting the living God.

Through this experience, doubts leave you, human thoughts and theories are destroyed, and you stand on the rock of faith in which you are never shaken by any kind of trials and afflictions. When you have become a man of truth and Christ-like at heart, it means that your foundation of faith is permanently laid. With this foundation of faith you can receive anything that you have asked for in that faith.

Just as our Lord Jesus said in Matthew 8:13, *"It shall be done for you as you have believed,"* if you come to possess complete spiritual faith, it is the faith by which you can receive anything that you have asked. You can lead a life of glorifying God in everything you do. You will dwell in the love and stronghold of God and become a great delight to God.

Now let's delve into a few things concerning spiritual faith. What are the obstacles to gaining spiritual faith? How can you possess spiritual faith? What kind of blessings did the fathers of spiritual faith receive in the Bible? And finally we will look at why those who set their minds on fleshly thoughts were forsaken.

Obstacles to Gaining Spiritual Faith

With the spiritual faith you can have communication with God. You can hear clear voice of the Holy Spirit. You can receive answers to your prayers and petitions. You can glorify God whether you eat or drink or whatever you do. And you will live in the favor, recognition and guarantee of God in your life.

Why then do people fail to possess spiritual faith? Now let's look into what kinds of factors hinder us from possessing spiritual faith.

1) Fleshly Thoughts

Romans 8:6-7 say, *"For the mind set on the flesh is death, but the mind set on the Spirit is life and peace, because the mind set on the flesh is hostile toward God; for it does not subject itself to the law of God, for it is not even able to do so."*

The mind can be divided into two parts; one that is fleshly in nature and one that is spiritual. The fleshly mind refers to all kinds of thoughts stored in the flesh, and consists of all kinds of untruths. Fleshly thoughts belong to sin because they are not according to the will of God. They give birth to death as said in Romans 6:23, *"The wages of sins is death."* On the contrary, the spiritual mind refers to the thoughts of truth, and is according to the will of God – righteousness and goodness. Spiritual thoughts give birth to life and bring peace on us.

For example, suppose you meet with a difficulty or a trial that cannot be overcome with human strength and ability. Fleshly thoughts bring you worries and anxieties. But spiritual thoughts lead you to cast off worries, and to give thanks and rejoice through the word of God saying, *"Rejoice always; pray without ceasing; in everything give thanks; for this is God's will for you in Christ Jesus"* (1 Thessalonians 5:16-18).

Thus, spiritual thoughts are exactly contrary to fleshly ones, so with fleshly thoughts you do not and cannot become subject to the law of God. That's why fleshly thoughts are hostile toward God and hinder us from possessing spiritual faith.

2) Deeds/Works of the Flesh

Deeds/works of the flesh refer to all sins and evils revealed in actions, just as defined in Galatians 5:19-21, *"Now the deeds of the flesh are evident, which are: immorality, impurity, sensuality, idolatry, sorcery, enmities, strife, jealousy, outbursts of anger, disputes, dissensions, factions, envying, drunkenness, carousing, and things like these, of which I forewarn you, just as I have forewarned you, that those who practice such things will not inherit the kingdom of God."*

If you do not throw away the deeds of the flesh, you can neither possess spiritual faith nor inherit the kingdom of God. That's why the works of the flesh prevent you from possessing spiritual faith.

3) All Kinds of Theories

The Webster's Revised Unabridged Dictionary refers to "Theory" as "A doctrine, or scheme of things, which terminates in speculation or contemplation, without a view to practice; hypothesis; speculation" or "An exposition of the general or abstract principles of any science." This idea of theory is a piece of knowledge that supports the creation of something from something, but is of no help to our possessing spiritual faith. It rather restricts us from possessing spiritual faith.

Let's think of the two theories of creationism and Darwinian evolutionism. Most of people learn in school that mankind has evolved from the ape. In direct opposition, the Bible tells us that God created man. If you believe in the almighty God, you have to choose and follow that creation was by God even if you have been taught the theory of evolution in school.

Only when you turn from the theory of evolution that has been taught in school to that of creation by God, can you possess spiritual faith. Otherwise, all theories hinder you from possessing spiritual faith because it is impossible for you to believe that something is made out of nothingness with the theory of evolution. For example, even with the development of science people cannot make the seeds of life, the sperm and egg. Then, how could it be possible to believe something is made out of nothingness unless it is within the aspects of spiritual faith?

Therefore, we must refute these arguments and theories, and every proud and lofty thing that sets itself up against the true knowledge of God, and make every thought captive and into the obedience of Christ.

Saul Follows Fleshly Thoughts and Disobeys

Saul was the first king of the kingdom of Israel, but he did not live in accordance with the will of God. He ascended to the throne at the request of the people. God commanded him to strike Amalek and utterly destroy all that he had and to put to death both man and woman, child and infant, ox and sheep, camel and donkey not sparing any of them at all. King Saul defeated the Amalekites and won the great triumph. But he did not obey the command of God, but spared the best of the sheep and oxen.

Saul acted according to fleshly thoughts, and spared Agag and the best of the sheep, the oxen, the fatlings, the lambs, and all that was good with a desire to sacrifice them to God. He was not willing to utterly destroy them all. This act was disobedience and arrogance in the sight of God. God reproached him for his wrongdoing through the prophet Samuel so that he might repent and turn back. But, King Saul made excuses and insisted on his righteousness (1 Samuel 15:2-21).

Today there are many believers who act like Saul. They do not realize their obvious disobediences, nor do they acknowledge when they are rebuked for them. Instead they make excuses and insist on their own ways according to their fleshly thoughts. In the end they are found to be men of disobedience who are according to the flesh like Saul. Since all 100 out of 100 people are different in their opinions, if they act according to their own thoughts, they cannot become united. If they act according to their own thoughts they will come to disobey. But if they act according to the truth of God, they will be able to obey and become united.

God sent Prophet Samuel to Saul. Saul had not obeyed His word and the Prophet said to Saul, *"For rebellion is as the sin of divination, and insubordination is as iniquity and idolatry. Because you have rejected the word of the LORD, He has also rejected you from being king"* (1 Samuel 15:23).

Likewise, if anyone relies on human thoughts and does not follow the will of God, it is disobedience to God, and if he does not realize his disobedience nor turns away from it, he has no other choice but to be forsaken by God like Saul.

In 1 Samuel 15:23, Samuel rebuked Saul saying, *"Has the LORD as much delight in burnt offerings and sacrifices as in obeying the voice of the LORD? Behold, to obey is better than sacrifice, and to heed than the fat of rams."* No matter how right your thoughts seem to be, if they are against the word of God, you have to repent of and turn away from them immediately. In addition, you have to make your thoughts obedient to the will of God.

Fathers of Faith Who Obeyed the Word of God

David was the second king of Israel. He did not follow his own thoughts since his childhood, but he walked only by the faith in God. He did not fear bears and lions when he shepherded the flock, and sometimes he wrestled against and defeated lions and bears by faith to protect the flock. Later with only faith, he defeated Goliath, the champion of the Philistines.

There was an incident where David once disobeyed the word of God after he sat on the throne. When he was rebuked by the prophet for it, he spoke no word of excuse, but immediately repented and turned away, and in the end he became more sanctified. Thus, there was a great difference between Saul, a man of fleshly thoughts, and David, a man of spirit (1 Samuel 12:13).

While he was shepherding the flocks in a desert for forty years, Moses destroyed all kinds of thoughts and theories and became humble before God until he could be called by God to lead the Israelites out of the bondage of Egypt.

Thinking according to human thought, Abraham called his wife, "sister." After he became a man of spirit through trials, however, he could obey even the command of God telling him to offer his only son Isaac as a burnt offering. Had he relied even a little bit on fleshly thought, he could not have obeyed the command at all. Isaac was his only son whom he had gained in his latter years, and also was to be the seed of the promise of God. So, with the human thoughts, it might be considered improper and impossible to cut him to pieces like an animal and offer him as a burnt offering. Abraham never complained but instead believed that God would be able to raise him from the dead and he obeyed (Hebrews 11:19).

Naaman, commander of the army of the king of Aram, was highly respected and favored by the king, but was found stricken with leprosy, and came to Prophet Elisha to receive the healing of his disease. Though he brought many presents to experience works of God, Elisha did not let him in, but instead sent his servant to tell him, *"Go and wash in the Jordan seven times, and your flesh will be restored to you and you will be clean"* (2 Kings 5:10). With fleshly thoughts, Naaman considered this rude and offensive and he became furious.

But he demolished his fleshly thoughts and obeyed the command at the advice given by his servants. He dipped himself in the Jordan River seven times, and his flesh was restored and he became clean.

Water symbolizes the word of God, and number 'seven' stands for the perfection, so 'dipping himself into the Jordan River seven times' means "to become completely sanctified by the word of God." When you become sanctified, you can receive the solution to any kind of problem. Thus, when Naaman obeyed the word of God prophesied by Prophet Elisha, amazing work of God took place to him (2 Kings 5:1-14).

Once You Dispel Human Thoughts and Theories You Can Obey

Jacob was crafty and had all kinds of thoughts, so he tried to accomplish his will with various schemes. As a result, he suffered many difficulties for twenty years. At last he fell into a predicament at the Jabbok River. He could not return to his uncle's house because of the covenant made with his uncle nor go forward because his elder brother, Esau, was waiting at the opposite side of the river to kill him. In this desperate situation his self-righteousness and all fleshly thoughts were completely destroyed. God moved the heart of Esau and reconciled him to his brother. In this way God opened the path to life so that Jacob would be able to fulfill the providence of God (Genesis 33:1-4).

God says in Romans 8:5-7, *"For those who are according to the flesh set their minds on the things of the flesh, but those who are according to the Spirit, the things of the Spirit. For the mind set on the flesh is death, but the mind set on the Spirit is life and peace, because the mind set on the flesh is hostile toward God; for it does not subject itself to the law of God, for it is not even able to do so."* That's why we have to destroy every opinion, every theory, and every thought that is raised in opposition to the knowledge of God. We must make every thought captive to the obedience of Christ so that we can be given spiritual faith and show the deeds of obedience.

Jesus gave a new commandment in Matthew 5:39-42 saying, *"But I say to you, do not resist an evil person; but whoever slaps you on your right cheek, turn the other to him also. If anyone wants to sue you and take your shirt, let him have your coat also. Whoever forces you to go one mile, go with him two. Give to him who asks of you, and do not turn away from him who wants to borrow from you."* With human thoughts you cannot obey this commandment because they are against the word of truth. But if you destroy human and fleshly thoughts, you can obey it with joy, and God will cause everything to work for the good for you through your obedience.

No matter how many times you profess your faith with your lips, unless you put your own thoughts and theories to nothingness, you can neither obey nor experience the works of God or be guided to prosperity and success.

I urge you to bear in your mind the word of God written in Isaiah 55:8-9, saying, *"'For My thoughts are not your thoughts, nor are your ways My ways,' declares the LORD. 'For as the heavens are higher than the earth, so are My ways higher than your ways and My thoughts than your thoughts.'"*

You have to avoid having all fleshly thoughts and human theories and instead possess spiritual faith like a centurion who was commended by Jesus for his complete reliance on God. When the centurion came to Jesus and asked Him to heal his servant whose whole body had been paralyzed because of a stroke, he confessed by faith that the servant would be healed just by the word spoken by Jesus. He received the answer as he had believed. In the same way, if you possess this spiritual faith, you can receive answers to all your prayers and petitions and fully give glory to God.

The word of truth of God converts the spirit of mankind

and enables him to possess the faith accompanied with actions. You can receive God's answers with this living and spiritual faith. May each of you demolish all fleshly thoughts and human theories and possess spiritual faith so that you can receive anything that you have asked for by faith and glorify God.

Chapter 4

Sow the Seeds of Faith

Galatians 6:6-10

The one who is taught the word is to share all good things with the one who teaches him. Do not be deceived, God is not mocked; for whatever a man sows, this he will also reap. For the one who sows to his own flesh will from the flesh reap corruption, but the one who sows to the Spirit will from the Spirit reap eternal life. Let us not lose heart in doing good, for in due time we will reap if we do not grow weary. So then, while we have opportunity, let us do good to all people, and especially to those who are of the household of the faith.

Jesus promises us in Mark 9:23, *"'If You can?' All things are possible to him who believes."* So when a centurion came to Him and showed such great faith, Jesus said to him, *"It shall be done for you as you have believed"* (Matthew 8:13), and then the servant was healed at that very moment.

This is the spiritual faith that lets us believe in what cannot be seen. And it is also the faith accompanied with deeds that enables us to reveal our faith with deeds. It is the faith to believe that something is made out of nothingness. That's why faith is defined as the following in Hebrews 11:1-3: *"Now faith is the assurance of things hoped for, the conviction of things not seen. For by it the men of old gained approval. By faith we understand that the worlds were prepared by the word of God, so that what is seen was not made out of things which are visible."*

If you possess spiritual faith, God will delight in your faith and allow you to receive whatever you have asked for. What then do we have to do in order to possess spiritual faith?

Just as a farmer sows seeds in spring and reaps their fruits in fall, we have to sow the seeds of faith to possess the fruit of spiritual faith.

Now let's look into how to sow the seed of faith through the parables of sowing the seeds and reaping their fruits from the field. Jesus spoke to the crowds in parables, and He did not speak to them without using parables (Matthew 13:34). It is because God is spirit and we, who live in this physical world as human beings, cannot understand the spiritual realm of God. Only when we are taught the spiritual realm with the parables of this physical world, will we be able to understand the true will of God. That's why I am going to explain to you how to sow the seeds of faith and to possess spiritual faith with some parables of the farming field.

To Plant the Seeds of Faith

1) First of all, you have to clear the field.

Above all else, a farmer needs a field to sow the seeds. In order to make his field suitable, the farmer has to apply proper fertilizers, turn over the ground, pick out stones, and break lumped earth into pieces in a process of cultivation including plowing, harrowing and tilling the soil. Only then, will the seeds sown into the field grow well and produce a harvest of many good fruits.

In the Bible Jesus introduced to us the four kinds of field. The field refers to the heart of men. The first category is the field at the path's edge in which the seeds sown cannot sprout because it is too solid; the second one is the rocky field in which the seeds sown are barely able to sprout or the few buds hardly grow because of stones in the field; the third is the thorny field in which the seeds sprout but fail to grow well and bear good fruits because thorns choke them out; the last and fourth one is the good field where the seeds sprout, grow well, produce blossoms and bear many good fruits.

In the same way, the field of the heart of men is categorized into four kinds; the first is the heart-field beside the path in which they cannot understand the word of God; the second is the heart-field of rocks in which they receive the word of God but fall away when trials and persecutions arise; the third is the heart-field of thorns in which the worries of the world and the deceitfulness of wealth choke out the word of God and prevent those who hear from bearing fruits; the last and fourth is the good heart-field in which they understand God's word and bear good fruits. But no matter what kind of heart-field you have, if you cultivate and cleanse the heart-field as a farmer toils and sweats in his field, your heart-field can be turned into a good one. If it is solid, you have to turn it over and make it smooth; if it is rocky, you have to pick the stones out; if it is thorny, you have to remove thorns and then you have to make it good soil by applying 'fertilizers.'

If the farmer is lazy, he cannot clear the field and make it a good one, while a diligent farmer does his best to reclaim and clear the land to make it a good field. And then as it turns into good field, it produces better fruits.

If you have faith, you will try your best to change your heart into a good one with toil and sweat. Then, in order for you to understand the word of God, make your heart a good one, and to bear many fruits, you need to struggle against and throw away your sins to the point of the shedding of blood. So, by diligently throwing away your sins and evils according to the word of God just as God commands us to get rid of every form of evil, you can remove each stone from your heart field, weed it out, and change it into a good one.

A farmer diligently toils and works because he believes that he will reap an abundant harvest if he plows, harrows and tills the soil and changes the field into good one. In the same way, I wish for you to believe that if you cultivate and change your heart-field into a good one, you will dwell in the love of God, be guided to success and prosperity and enter the better place of heaven, and to struggle against and throw away your sins to the point of shedding blood. Then, into your heart will the seed of spiritual faith be planted and you bear as many fruits as you are able.

2) Next, the seeds are necessary.

After clearing the field, you have to sow the seeds and help the seeds sprout. A farmer sows various kinds of seeds and reaps abundant fruits of various kinds such as cabbage, lettuce, pumpkin, green beans, red beans, and the like.

In the same way, we have to sow various kinds of seeds into our heart-fields. The word of God tells us to rejoice always, pray without ceasing, give thanks in everything, give whole tithes, keep the Lord's Day holy, and love. When these words of God are planted into your heart, they will sprout, put forth buds, and grow producing spiritual fruit. You will be able to live by the word of God and possess spiritual faith.

3) Water and sunlight are necessary.

For a farmer to reap good harvest, it is not enough for him to just clear the field and prepare seeds. Water and sunlight are necessary as well. Only then, will the seeds sprout and grow well.

What does the water represent?

Jesus says in John 4:14, *"Whoever drinks of the water that I will give him shall never thirst; but the water that I will give him will become in him a well of water springing up to eternal life."* Water spiritually refers to "water springing up to eternal life," and eternal water refers to the word of God as recorded in John 6:63, *"The words that I have spoken to you are spirit and are life."* That's why Jesus said in John 6:53-55, *"Truly, truly, I say to you, unless you eat the flesh of the Son of Man and drink His blood, you have no life in yourselves. He who eats My flesh and drinks My blood has eternal life, and I will raise him up on the last day. For My flesh is true food, and My blood is true drink."* Accordingly, only when you diligently read, listen to and mediate on the word of God and earnestly pray with it, will you be able to go the way of eternal life and possess spiritual faith.

Next, what does it mean by the sunlight?

The sunlight helps seeds sprout properly and grow well. By the same token, if the word of God enters into your heart, then the word that is the light drives out darkness from the heart. It purifies your heart and turns the heart field into a good one. So, you can possess spiritual faith to the extent to which the light of truth fills your heart.

Through a parable of farming, we have learned that we have to clear the heart-field, prepare good seeds, and provide proper water and sunlight as the seeds of faith are planted. Next, let's look into how to plant the seeds of faith and how to raise them.

How to Plant and Raise the Seeds of Faith

1) First of all, you have to sow the seeds of faith according to Gods' ways.

A farmer sows the seeds differently according to what kind of seed it is. He plants some seeds deep into the soil, while some others are planted shallowly. In the same way, you have to vary the ways of sowing the seeds of faith with the word of God. For example, when you sow prayers, you have to cry out with a sincere heart and on a regular basis kneeling down as explained according to the word of God. Only then will you be able to receive God's answers (Luke 22:39-46).

2) Secondly, you have to sow with faith.

Just as a farmer is diligent and fervent when he sows the seeds because he believes and hopes that he will be able to reap, you have to sow the seeds of faith – the word of God – with joy and the hope that God will let you reap abundantly. So, in 2 Corinthians 9:6-7, He encourages us, saying, *"Now this I say, he who sows sparingly will also reap sparingly, and he who sows bountifully will also reap bountifully. Each one must do just as he has purposed in his heart, not grudgingly or under compulsion, for God loves a cheerful giver."*

It is the law of this world and the law of the spiritual realm that we should reap whatever we have sown. So, as much as your faith grows, your heart field will become better. As you sow more you will reap more. Therefore, whatever kind of seed you sow you must sow it with faith, thanksgiving and joy so that you can harvest abundant fruit.

3) Thirdly, you have to take good care of the sprouted seeds.

After the farmer has prepared the land and has sown the seeds, he has to water the plants in season, prevent worm and insect damage by spraying insecticide, continue to fertilize the field, and pull out the weeds. Otherwise they will wither and cannot grow. When the word of God has been planted, it also has to be cultivated to keep the enemy devil and Satan from drawing near. One must cultivate it with fervent prayer, hold onto it with joy and thanksgiving, attend worship services, share in Christian fellowship, read and hear the word of God and serve. Then the sown seed can sprout, blossom and bear fruit.

The Process in Which Flowers Come out and Fruits Are Borne

Unless a farmer takes care of the seeds after sowing them, worms eat them, and weeds thrive, and hinder the seeds from growing and bearing fruits. The farmer should not become weary of his work but patiently raise the plants until he harvests good and abundant fruits. When proper time comes, the seeds grow, blossom, and finally bear fruits through bees and butterflies. When the fruits ripen, the farmer can finally reap good fruits joyfully. How joyous he will be when all his labors and patience turn into good and valuable fruits with the harvest of thirty, sixty, or a hundred times what he planted!

1) First, the spiritual flower blossoms.

What does it mean that 'The seeds of faith grow and put forth spiritual blossoms'? If the flowers blossom, they give off fragrance, and the fragrance brings bees and butterflies. In the same way, when we have sown the seeds of the word of God into our heart-field and they are cared for, to the extent that we live according to the word of God we can put forth spiritual blossoms and spread the fragrance of Christ. In addition we are able to play the role of the light and salt of the world so that many people may see our good works and glorify our heavenly Father (Matthew 5:16).

If you send out the fragrance of Christ, the enemy devil will be driven out and you will be able to glorify God in your homes, businesses, and places of work. Whether you are eating or drinking or whatever you do, you can glorify God. As a result, you will bear the fruits of evangelism, accomplish the kingdom and righteousness of God, and change into a man of spirit by clearing your heart-field and make it good one.

2) Next, the fruits are borne and ripen.

After the flowers blossom, fruits begin to be borne and when the fruits become ripe, the farmer harvests them. If we apply this to our faith, what kind of fruit can we bear? We can bear various kinds of fruits of the Holy Spirit including the nine fruits of the Holy Spirit as recorded in Galatians 5:22-

23, the fruits of the Beatitudes in Matthew 5, and the fruits of spiritual love as written in 1 Corinthians 13.

Through the reading of the Bible and the listening to the word of God, we can examine if we have produced blossoms, and borne fruits and how ripe the fruits are. When the fruits are fully ripe, we can harvest them at any time and enjoy them as necessary. Psalm 37:4 says, *"Delight yourself in the LORD; and He will give you the desires of your heart."* It is much the same as depositing billions of dollars in a bank account and being able to spend that money in any way one desires.

3) Lastly, you will reap as you have sown.

Whenever in season, a farmer reaps whatever he has sowed, and he repeats this every year. Here the amount of his harvest is different according to how much he has sown and how fervently and faithfully he has tended the seeds.

If you have sown in prayer, your spirit will prosper, and if you have sown in loyalty and service, you will enjoy good health in spirit and body. If you have diligently sown in finance, you will enjoy financial blessing and help the poor with charity as much as you want. God promises us in Galatians 6:7, *"Do not be deceived, God is not mocked; for whatever a man sows, this he will also reap."*

Many parts of the Bible confirm this promise of God saying that a man who sows will reap as sown. In the seventeenth chapter of 1 Kings is the story of a widow living at Zarephath. Because there had been no rain in the land and the brook dried up, she and her son were at the point of starvation. But she sowed a handful of flour in a bowl with a little oil from the jar for Elijah, a man of God. At that time when food was more valuable than gold, it was not possible for her to do it without faith. She believed and relied on the word of God that had been prophesied through Elijah, and sowed it with faith. God gave her amazing blessing in return for her faith, and she, her son and Elijah could eat until the long famine finally came to an end (1 Kings 17:8-16).

Mark 12:41-44 introduces to us about a poor widow who put two small copper coins, which amount to a cent, into the treasury. What a great blessing she received when Jesus commended her action!

God has set the law of the spiritual realm and tells us that we can reap as we have sown. But I urge you to remember that it is mocking God for you to want to reap when you have not sown. You have to believe that God will let you reap thirty, sixty, or a hundred times more than what you sow.

Through the parable of a farmer, we have looked into how to plant the seeds of faith and how to raise it in order to possess spiritual faith. Now I wish for you to reclaim your heart-field and make it a good one. Sow the seeds of faith and cultivate them. Thus, you have to sow as much as possible and raise them with faith and hope and patience so as to receive the blessing thirty, sixty, or a hundred times. When the proper time comes, you will reap fruits and give great glory to God.

May each of you believe in every word of the Bible and sow the seeds of faith according to the teachings of the word of God so that you may bear abundant fruits, glorify God and enjoy all kinds of blessings!

Chapter 5

'If You can?'
All Things Are Possible!

Mark 9:21-27

And [Jesus] asked his father, "How long has this been happening to him?" And he said, "From childhood. It has often thrown him both into the fire and into the water to destroy him. But if You can do anything, take pity on us and help us!" And Jesus said to him, "'If You can?' All things are possible to him who believes." Immediately the boy's father cried out and said, "I do believe; help my unbelief." When Jesus saw that a crowd was rapidly gathering, He rebuked the unclean spirit, saying to it, "You deaf and mute spirit, I command you, come out of him and do not enter him again." After crying out and throwing him into terrible convulsions, it came out; and the boy became so much like a corpse that most of them said, "He is dead!" But Jesus took him by the hand and raised him; and he got up.

Men store their life's experiences through the impressions of all they go through including joys, sorrows, and pains. Many of them sometimes meet with and suffer serious problems that they cannot solve with tears, endurance, or help from others.

These are problems of diseases that cannot be cured with modern medicines; mental problems from stress of life that cannot be unraveled with any kind of philosophy or psychology; problems of home and children that cannot be solved with the greatest amounts of wealth; problems in business and finances that cannot be fulfilled by any means or efforts. And the list goes on. Who can solve all these problems?

In Mark 9:21-27, we find the conversation of Jesus and the father of a child who was possessed by evil spirits. The child seriously suffered from both deaf-muteness and epileptic seizures. He often hurled himself into the water and into the fire because of the demon-possession. Whenever demons seized him, they slammed him to the ground and he foamed at the mouth, and ground his teeth and stiffened out.

Now let's look into how the farther received the solution to the problem from Jesus.

Jesus Reproached the Father for His Unbelief

The child had been deaf and mute since his birth and so he couldn't hear anybody and he had serious difficulty in making himself understood by anyone else. He was often tormented by epilepsy and showed the symptoms in convulsions. That's why the father had to live in midst of pains and anxiety and had no hope in life.

In time the father heard about the news of Jesus who had brought the dead back to life, healed the sick of all kinds of diseases, opened the sight of the blind, and performed various miracles. The news planted hope into the father's heart. He thought, "If he had the same power as I have heard, he might be able to heal my son of all his disease." He suspected that his son's healing might have a chance of occurring. Just with this expectation he brought his son to Jesus and petitioned Him, saying, "If You can do anything, take pity on us and help us!"

When Jesus heard him, He reproached him for unbelief, saying to him, "'If You can?' All things are possible to him who believes." It was because the father heard about Jesus, but did not believe in Him from the heart.

If the father had believed that Jesus is the Son of God and the Almighty with whom nothing is impossible, and the Truth Himself, he would never have said to Him, "If You can do anything, take pity on us and help us!"

Without faith it is impossible to please God, and without spiritual faith it is not possible to receive answers. In order that

Jesus might let the father realize this fact, He said to the father, "If you can?" and rebuked him that he did not fully believe.

How to Possess Complete Faith

When you believe in what cannot be seen, your faith can be accepted by God, and the faith is called 'spiritual faith,' 'true faith,' 'living faith' or 'faith accompanied with actions.' By this faith you can believe that something is made out of nothingness. It is because faith is the assurance of things hoped for and the conviction of things not seen (Hebrews 11:1).

You have to believe from the heart the way of the cross, resurrection, the return of the Lord, the creation of God, and miracles. Only then can you be deemed to have complete faith. When you confess the faith with your lips, it is true confession.

There are three conditions to fully possess complete faith.

First of all, the barrier of sins against God must be destroyed. If you find yourself having a barrier of sins, you have to destroy it by repenting of them. Additionally, you have to struggle against your sins to the point of shedding blood and avoid every form of evil not to commit any sin at all. If you hate sins to the point of feeling troubled just with the thought of sins and becoming nervous and anxious at the sight of sins, how could you dare to sin? Instead of living a life of sin you can communicate with God and possess complete faith.

Second, you have to follow the will of God. In order to do the will of God, first of all, you have to clearly understand what the will of God is. Then, no matter what you may personally desire, if it is not the will of God, you should not do it. On the other hand, whatever it might be that you don't want to do, if it is the will of God, you have to do it. When you follow His will with all your heart, sincerity, strength and wisdom, He gives you complete faith.

Third, you have to please God with the love for Him. If you do all things for glory of God, whether you are eating or drinking or whatever you do, and if you please God even by sacrificing yourself, you never fail to possess complete faith. It is that faith that makes possible what is impossible. With this complete faith, you come to believe not only what is seen and possible to accomplish with your strength, but also what is unseen and impossible with human abilities. Thus, when you confess this complete faith, everything impossible will be made possible.

Accordingly, the word of God saying, "'If You can?' All things are possible to him who believes" will come upon you and you can glorify Him in whatever you do.

Nothing Is Impossible to Him Who Believes

When complete faith is given to you, nothing is impossible to you and you can receive solutions to any kind of problems. In what areas can you experience the power of God who makes the impossible possible? Let's look into three kinds of aspects.

The first field of the three is the problems of diseases.

Suppose you are sick because of bacterial or viral infection. If you show the faith and are filled with the Holy Spirit, the fire of the Holy Spirit will burn those diseases and you be healed. More detailed, if you repent of your sins and turn away from them, you can be healed through prayers. If you are a beginner of faith, you have to open your heart and listen to the word of God until you are able to show your faith.

Next, if you are stricken with serious diseases that cannot be cured with medical treatments, you have to show the proof of great faith. Only when you thoroughly repent of your sins by rending your heart and cling to God through tearful prayers, can you be healed. But those who have weak faith or those who have just started attending church cannot be healed until spiritual faith is given them, and as far as that faith comes upon them, healing works happen to them little by little.

Lastly, physical deformities, abnormalities, lameness,

deafness, mentally and physically handicapping conditions, and hereditary problems cannot be restored without the power of God. Those who suffer such conditions have to show their sincerity before God and present the proof of the faith to love and please Him so that they can be recognized by God and then the healing works can occur with them through the power of God.

Those healing works can happen to them only when they show the deeds of faith just the way a blind beggar named Bartimaeus cried out to Jesus (Mark 10:46-52), a centurion revealed his great faith (Matthew 8:6-13), and a paralytic and his four friends presented the proof of their faith before Jesus (Mark 2:3-12).

The second field is the problems of finance.

If you try to solve the problem of finance with your knowledge, ways, and experiences without the help of God, the problem can be solved only according to your abilities and efforts. However, if you throw off your sins, follow the will of God, and commit your problem to God believing that God will lead you in His way, your soul will prosper, everything go well with you and you enjoy good health. Furthermore, because you walk in the Holy Spirit, you receive the blessings of God.

Jacob had followed human ways and wisdom in his life until he wrestled with the angel of God at the River Jabbok. The angel touched the socket of his thigh and the socket of his thigh was dislocated. In this wrestling with the angel of God, he submitted himself to God and left everything to Him. From that time on he received the blessing of God being with him. In the same way, if you love God, please Him, and commit everything into His hands, everything will go well with you.

The third is concerning how to receive spiritual strength.

We find in 1 Corinthians 4:20 that the kingdom of God does not consist in words but in power. Power becomes greater as much as we come to possess complete faith. The power of God comes upon us differently according to our measure of prayers, faith and love. The works of the miracles of God, which is at a higher level than the gift of healing, can be performed only by those who receive God's power through prayers and fasting.

Thus, if you possess complete faith, the impossible will be possible to you and you can courageously confess, "'If You can?' All things are possible to him who believes."

"I do believe; help my unbelief!"

There is a process necessary for you to receive the solutions to any kind of problem.

First, to start the process you must offer positive confessions with your lips.

There was a father who had been in aguish for a long time because his son was possessed with evil spirits. When the father heard about Jesus, he came to have a longing heart to see Him. Later the father brought his son to Jesus expecting that there might be a chance that his son could possibly be healed. Even though he did not have the assurance of it, he asked Jesus to heal his son.

Jesus rebuked the father for saying, "If You can?" But then He encouraged him saying, "All things are possible to him who believes." At this word of encouragement, the father cried out and said, "I do believe; help my unbelief." Thus, he made this positive confession before Jesus.

Because he heard just with his ears that *all things are possible with Jesus,* he understood it in his brain and confessed his faith only with his lips, but did not confess the faith that could make him believe from the heart. Even though he had faith as knowledge, his positive confession became an urging of spiritual faith and led him to receive the answer.

Next, you have to possess spiritual faith that makes you believe from your heart.

The father of the demon-possessed child eagerly longed to receive spiritual faith, and said to Jesus, *"I do believe; help my unbelief"* (Mark 9:23). When Jesus heard the father's request, He knew the father's sincere heart, truthfulness, earnest petition, and faith, and so He gave him spiritual faith that let him believe from his heart. Thus, because the father came to possess spiritual faith, God could work for him and he received an answer from God.

When Jesus commanded in Mark 9:25, *"You deaf and mute spirit, I command you, come out of him and do not enter him again,"* the evil spirit came out.

In a word, the boy's father could not receive God's answer with fleshly faith that was stored merely as knowledge. But, as soon as he came to receive spiritual faith, God's answer was immediately given to him.

The third point in the process is to cry out in prayer until the last moment of receiving the answers.

In Jeremiah 33:3, God promises us, *"Call to Me and I will answer you, and I will tell you great and mighty things, which you do not know,"* and in Ezekiel 36:36, He teaches us, *"This also I will let the house of Israel ask Me to do for them."* As written as above, Jesus, prophets of the Old Testament, and disciples of the New Testament cried out and prayed to God to receive His answers.

By the same token, only through the crying out in prayer can you receive the faith that lets you believe from the heart and only through that spiritual faith can you receive the answers to prayers and problems. You have to cry out in prayers until you receive answers, and then the impossible will be possible for you. The father of a demon-possessed child could receive the answer because he cried out to Jesus.

This story of the father of a demon-possessed child gives us an important lesson in the law of God. In order for us to experience the word of God saying, "'If You can?' All things are possible to him who believes," you have to turn your fleshly faith into spiritual faith that helps you possess complete faith, stand on the rock, and obey without doubts.

To sum up the process, first you need to make the positive confession with your fleshly faith that is stored as knowledge. Then you must cry out to God in prayers until you receive answers. And finally you have to receive the spiritual faith from above that makes it possible for you to believe from your heart.

And, to meet the three conditions to receive complete answers, first destroy the wall of sins against God. Next, show the actions of faith with sincerity. Then let your soul prosper. As much as you fulfill these three conditions, you will be given spiritual faith from above and make possible what is impossible.

If you try to do things by yourself instead of committing them to the almighty God, you will have troubles and meet with difficulties. On the contrary, if you destroy human thoughts that make you consider it impossible and leave everything to God, He will do everything for you, so what will be impossible?

Fleshly thoughts are hostile against God (Romans 8:7). They hinder you from believing and cause you to disappoint God by making negative confessions. They help Satan bring accusations against you and also bring tests, trials, troubles and difficulties upon you. Therefore, you have to destroy these fleshly thoughts. No matter what kind of problems you meet with, including the problems of your soul's prosperity, business, works, diseases, and family, you have to commit them into the hands of God. You have to rely on the almighty God, believe that He will make possible what is impossible, and destroy all kinds of fleshly thoughts by faith.

When you make positive confessions saying "I believe," and pray to God from the heart, God will give you the faith that helps you believe from the heart, and with this faith He will let you receive the answers to any kind of problems and glorify Him. What a blessed life this is!

May you walk only in the faith in order to accomplish the kingdom and righteousness of God, to fulfill the Great Commission of preaching the gospel to the world, and to do the will of God assigned to you, and make the impossible possible as a soldier of the cross, and shine the light of Christ, in the name of Jesus Christ I pray!

Chapter 6

Daniel Relied only on God

Daniel 6:21-23

Then Daniel spoke to the king, "O king, live forever! My God sent His angel and shut the lions' mouths and they have not harmed me, inasmuch as I was found innocent before Him; and also toward you, O king, I have committed no crime." Then the king was very pleased and gave orders for Daniel to be taken up out of the den. So Daniel was taken up out of the den and no injury whatever was found on him, because he had trusted in his God.

When he was a child, Daniel was taken away into slavery in Babylonia. But later, he sat in the position of the king's favor as second to the king. Because he loved God to the utmost degree, God bestowed on him knowledge and intelligence in every branch of literature and wisdom. Daniel even understood all kinds of visions and dreams. He was a politician and prophet who revealed the power of God.

During his whole lifetime, Daniel never compromised with the world in serving God. He overcame all trials and tests with the faith of martyrdom and glorified God with great triumphs of faith. What are we to do in order to possess the same faith as he did?

Let's delve into why Daniel, who was next to the king as the ruler in Babylonia, was cast into the lions' den and how he survived in the lions' den without a single scratch on his body.

Daniel, Man of Faith

At the reign of King Rehoboam, the United Kingdom of Israel was divided into two – the Southern Kingdom of Judah and the Northern Kingdom of Israel because of King Solomon's degradation (1 Kings 11:26-36). The kings and the nation that obeyed the commands of God were prosperous but those who disobeyed the law of God were put to destruction.

In 722 B.C. the Northern Kingdom of Israel collapsed under the attack of Assyria. At the time countless numbers of people were taken captive into Assyria. The Southern Kingdom of Judah was also invaded, but was not destroyed.

Later King Nebuchadnezzar attacked the Southern Kingdom of Judah, and on the third attempt he broke down the city of Jerusalem and destroyed the temple of God. It was in 586 B.C.

In the third year of the reign of Jehoiakim, the king of Judah, Nebuchadnezzar, king of Babylon came to Jerusalem and besieged it. At this first attack, King Nebuchadnezzar bound King Jehoiakim with bronze chains to take him to Babylon, and also brought some of the articles of the house of God to Babylon.

Daniel was among the royal family and nobles taken as the first captives. They lived in the Gentile land, yet Daniel prospered while serving several kings - Nebuchadnezzar and Belshazzar, who were kings of Babylon, and Darius and Cyrus, who were the kings of Persia. Daniel lived in the Gentile countries for a long time and served the countries as one of the rulers after the kings. But he showed the faith by which he did not compromise with the world and led a triumphant life as a prophet of God.

Nebuchadnezzar, king of Babylon ordered the chief of his officials to bring in some of the sons of Israel, including some of the royal family and of the nobles, youths in whom was no defect, who were good-looking, showing intelligence in every branch of wisdom, endowed with understanding and discerning knowledge, and who had ability for serving in the king's court; and he ordered him to teach them the literature and language of the Chaldeans, and let them have the king's choice food and the wine which he drank, and appointed that they should be educated three years. Daniel was one of them (Daniel 1:4-5).

But Daniel made up his mind that he would not defile himself with the king's choice food or with the wine which he drank; so he sought permission from the commander of the officials that he might not defile himself (Daniel 1:8). This was the faith of Daniel who wanted to keep the law of God. Now God granted Daniel favor and compassion in the sight of the commander of the officials (v. 9). So the overseer continued to withhold his and his friends' choice food and the wine they were to drink, and kept giving them vegetables (v. 16).

Since He saw the faith of Daniel, God gave him knowledge and intelligence in every branch of literature and wisdom; Daniel even understood all kinds of visions and dreams (v. 17). As for every matter of wisdom and understanding about which the king consulted him, he found him ten times better than all the magicians and conjurers who were in all his realm (v. 20).

Later King Nebuchadnezzar was troubled of his dream that he had dreamed and couldn't sleep, and none of the Chaldeans could interpret his dream. But Daniel succeeded in interpreting it by the wisdom and power of God. Then the king promoted

Daniel and gave him many great gifts, and he made him ruler over the whole province of Babylon and chief prefect over all the wise men of Babylon (Daniel 2: 46-48).

Not only in the reign of Nebuchadnezzar king of Babylon but also in the reign of Belshazzar did Daniel gain favor and recognition. King Belshazzar issued a proclamation that Daniel had authority as the third ruler in the kingdom. When King Belshazzar was killed and Darius became the king, Daniel was still in the favor of the king.

King Darius appointed 120 satraps over the kingdom and over them three commissioners. But since Daniel began distinguishing himself among the commissioners and satraps with his extraordinary spirit, the king planned to appoint him over the entire kingdom.

Then the commissioners and satraps began trying to find a ground of accusation against Daniel in regard to government affairs; but they could find no ground of accusation or evidence of corruption, inasmuch as he was faithful, and no negligence or corruption was to be found in him. They plotted a scheme to find the ground of accusation against Daniel with regard to the law of God. They requested that the king should establish a statute and enforce an injunction that anyone who would make a petition to any god or man besides the king for thirty days should be cast into the lions' den. And they requested that the king establish the injunction and sign the document so that it may not be changed according to the law of the Medes and

Persians which may not be revoked. Therefore King Darius signed the document, that is, the injunction.

When Daniel knew that the document was signed, he entered his house and in his roof chamber he had windows open toward Jerusalem; and he continued kneeling on his knees three times a day, praying and giving thanks before his God, as he had been doing previously (Daniel 6:10). Daniel knew that he should be cast into the lions' den if he were to violate the injunction, but determined for a martyred death and served God alone.

Even in the midst of the captivity in Babylon, Daniel always remembered the grace of God and fervently loved Him to the point of kneeling to the ground, praying and giving thanks to Him three times a day without ceasing. He had strong faith and never compromised with the world in serving God.

Daniel Thrown Into the Lions' Den

The people who were jealous of Daniel came to an agreement and found Daniel making petition and supplication before his God. Then they approached and spoke before the king about the king's injunction. At last the king realized that the people had requested him to establish the injunction not because of the king himself but because of their scheme of removing Daniel, and was so surprised. But because the king had signed on the document and proclaimed the injunction, he himself could not overturn it.

As soon as the king heard this statement, he was deeply distressed and set his mind on delivering Daniel. But the commissioners and satraps compelled the king to enforce the injunction, and the king had no other choice but to do it.

The king was compelled to give orders, and Daniel was cast into the lions' den and a stone was brought and laid over the mouth of the den. This was because nothing would be changed in regard to Daniel.

Then the king, who had favored Daniel, went off to his palace and spent the night fasting, and no entertainment was brought before him; and his sleep fled from him. Then the king arose at dawn, at the break of day, and went in haste to the lions' den. It was naturally expected that since Daniel had been thrown into the hungry lions' den, he had been eaten by the lions. But the king went in haste to the lions' den expecting that he might survive.

At that time many condemned criminals were cast into the lions' den. But how could Daniel overcome the hungry lions and survive there? The king thought in his mind that the God whom Daniel had served might be able to save him, and came near the den. The king cried out with a troubled voice, spoke and said to Daniel, "Daniel, servant of the living God, has your God, whom you constantly serve, been able to deliver you from the lions?"

To his amazement, the voice of Daniel was heard from the inside of the lions' den. Daniel spoke to the king, *"O king, live forever! My God sent His angel and shut the lions' mouths and they have not harmed me, inasmuch as I was found innocent before Him; and also toward you, O king, I have committed no crime"* (Daniel 6:21-22).

Then the king was very pleased and gave orders for Daniel to be taken up out of the den. When Daniel was taken up out of the den, no injury whatsoever was found on him. How amazing this was! This was the great triumph that was performed by the faith of Daniel who had trusted in God! Because Daniel trusted in the living God, he survived in the midst of the hungry lions and revealed the glory of God even to the Gentiles.

And the king gave orders, and they brought those men who had maliciously accused Daniel, and they cast them, their children and their wives into the lions' den; and they had not reached the bottom of the den before the lions overpowered them and crushed all their bones (Daniel 6:24). Then Darius the king wrote to all the peoples, nations and men of every language who were living in all the land and let them fear God revealing to them who God is.

The king declared to them, *"May your peace abound! I make a decree that in all the dominion of my kingdom men are to fear and tremble before the God of Daniel; For He is the living God and enduring forever, and His kingdom is one which will not be destroyed, and His dominion will be forever. He delivers and rescues and performs signs and wonders in heaven and on earth, who has also delivered Daniel from the power of the lions"* (Daniel 6:26-27).

How great this triumph of faith is! All this was because no sin was found in Daniel and he fully trusted in God. If we walk in the word of God and dwell in His love, in no matter what kind of situation and condition, God will provide you with the way to escape and cause you to triumph.

Daniel, Victor of Great Faith

What kind of faith did Daniel possess that he could give such a great glory to God? Let's look into the kind of faith Daniel had so that we can overcome any kind of trials and afflictions and reveal the glory of the living God to many people.

First of all, Daniel never compromised his faith with anything of the world whatsoever.

He was in charge of general affairs of the country as one of the commissioners of Babylon, and was well aware that he would be cast into the lions' den if he were to break the injunction. But he never followed human thought and wisdom. He was not afraid of the people who had plotted schemes against him. He knelt down on the ground and prayed to God as he had previously done. If he had followed human thought, during the thirty days when the injunction was in effect he could have ceased praying to God or prayed in a secret room. Daniel, however, did not do either of the two. He did not seek to spare his life at all nor did he compromise with the world. He only kept his faith with his love for God.

In a word, it was because he had the faith of martyrdom that, even though he knew that the document had been signed, he entered his house, and in his roof chamber he had windows open toward Jerusalem. He continued to kneel three times a day, praying and giving thanks before his God, as he had been doing previously.

Secondly, Daniel had the faith in which he did not cease praying.

When he fell into the situation in which he had to prepare for his death, he prayed to God as had been usual for him. He did not want to commit the sin of ceasing to pray (1 Samuel 12:23).

Prayers are the breath of our spirits, so we should not cease to pray. When trials and afflictions come upon us, we have to pray, and when we are at peace, we have to pray so that we may not enter into temptations (Luke 22:40). Because he did not cease to pray, Daniel could keep his faith and overcome the trials.

Thirdly, Daniel had the faith in which he gave thanks in any circumstances.

Many fathers of faith recorded in the Bible gave thanks in everything by faith because they knew that it is true faith to give thanks in any circumstances. When Daniel was cast into the lions' den, because he followed the law of God, it became a triumph of faith. Even if he had been eaten by the lions, he would have been put into the arms of God and have lived in the everlasting kingdom of God. No matter what the outcome was to be, there was no fear for him! If a person completely believes in heaven, he cannot be afraid of death.

Even if Daniel were to live in peace as the ruler over the kingdom after the king, it would be merely a temporal honor. But if he were to keep his faith and die a martyr's death, he would be recognized by God, considered as the great in the kingdom of heaven and live in the everlasting shining glory. That's why the only thing he did was to give thanks.

Fourthly, Daniel never sinned. He had the faith by which he followed and practiced the word of God.

With regard to government affairs there were no grounds for accusation against Daniel. There was no trace of corruption, negligence or dishonesty to be found in him. How pure his life was!

Daniel did not feel regret and had no ill-feeling against the king who had ordered him to be cast into the lions' den. Instead he was still faithful to the king to the point of speaking to him saying, "O king, live forever!" If this test had been given him because he committed sins, God could not have protected him. But because Daniel did not sin, he could be protected by God.

Fifthly, Daniel had the faith in which he fully trusted in God alone.

If we have reverent fear of God and completely rely on Him, and we put our every affair into His hands, He will solve all kinds of problems for us. Daniel fully trusted in God and completely relied on Him. So, he did not compromise with the world but chose the law of God and asked for God's help. God saw Daniel's faith and made everything work for the good for him. Blessings were added to blessings so that great glory could be given to God.

If we have the same faith as Daniel had, no matter what kind of trials and difficulties we meet with, we can overcome them, turn them into the chances of blessings and bear witnesses to the living God. The enemy devil is prowling around to search for someone to devour. So, we have to resist the devil with the strong faith and live in the protection of God by keeping and abiding by the word of God.

Through trials that come upon us and last for a moment, God will perfect, confirm, strengthen and establish us (1 Peter 5:10). May you possess the same as Daniel's faith, walk with God all the time, and glorify Him, in the name of our Lord Jesus Christ I pray!

Chapter 7

God Provides in Advance

Genesis 22:11-14

But the angel of the LORD called to him from heaven and said, "Abraham, Abraham!" And he said, "Here I am." He said, "Do not stretch out your hand against the lad, and do nothing to him; for now I know that you fear God, since you have not withheld your son, your only son, from Me." Then Abraham raised his eyes and looked, and behold, behind him a ram caught in the thicket by his horns; and Abraham went and took the ram and offered him up for a burnt offering in the place of his son. Abraham called the name of that place The LORD Will Provide, as it is said to this day, "In the mount of the LORD it will be provided."

Jehovah-jireh! How exciting and pleasing it is just to hear it! It means that God prepares for everything in advance. Today many believers in God have heard and know that God works for, prepares for and leads us in advance. But most people fail to experience this word of God in their believing lives.

The word "Jehovah-jireh" is that of blessing, righteousness, and hope. Everyone desires and longs for these things. If we don't realize the path this word refers to, we cannot enter into the way of blessing. So, I wish to share with you the faith of Abraham as the example of a man who received the blessing of "Jehovah-jireh."

Abraham Put the Word of God First above Everything

Jesus says in Mark 12:30, *"You shall love the Lord your God with all your heart, and with all your soul, and with all your mind, and with all your strength."* As described in Genesis 22:11-14, Abraham loved God to such degree that he could communicate with God face to face, realized the will of God, and received the blessing of Jehovah-jireh. You should realize that it was not accidental at all for him to have received all this.

Abraham placed God first above everything, and considered His word as more valuable than anything else. So, he did not follow his own thoughts and he was always ready to obey

God. Because he was truthful to God and himself without any falsehood, he was prepared in the depths of his heart to receive the blessings.

God said to Abraham in Genesis 12:1-3, *"Go forth from your country, and from your relatives and from your father's house, to the land which I will show you; and I will make you a great nation, and I will bless you, and make your name great; and so you shall be a blessing; and I will bless those who bless you, and the one who curses you I will curse. And in you all the families of the earth will be blessed."*

In this situation, if Abraham had used human thought, he would have felt a little troubled when God commanded him to go forth from his country, his relatives and his father's house. But he considered God the Father, the Creator, as the first. In doing so he could obey and follow the will of God. In the same way, anyone can obey God with joy if he really loves God. It is because he believes that God causes everything to work for the good for him.

Many parts of the Bible show us many fathers of faith who considered the word of God as the first and walked according to His word. 1 Kings 19:20-21 say, *"[Elisha] left the oxen and ran after Elijah and said, 'Please let me kiss my father and my mother, then I will follow you.' And he said to him, 'Go back again, for what have I done to you?' So he returned from following him, and took the pair of oxen and sacrificed them and boiled their flesh with the implements of the oxen, and gave it to the people and they ate. Then he arose and followed Elijah and ministered to him."* When God called Elisha through Elijah, he immediately abandoned everything he had and followed after the will of God.

It was the same with the disciples of Jesus. When Jesus called them, they immediately followed Him. Matthew 4:18-22 tell us, *"Now as Jesus was walking by the Sea of Galilee, He saw two brothers, Simon who was called Peter, and Andrew his brother, casting a net into the sea; for they were fishermen. And He said to them, 'Follow Me, and I will make you fishers of men.' Immediately they left their nets and followed Him. Going on from there He saw two other brothers, James the son of Zebedee, and John his brother, in the boat with Zebedee their father, mending their nets; and He called them. Immediately they left the boat and their father, and followed Him."*

That's why I eagerly urge you to possess the faith by which you can obey whatever the will of God may be, and to consider the word of God as the first so that God can work for the good of everything for you by His power.

Abraham Always Responded, "Amen!"

According to the word of God, Abraham left his country, Haran, and went down into the land of Canaan. But because famine was so serious there, he had to move into the land of Egypt (Genesis 12:10). When he moved into there, Abraham called his wife his 'sister' to keep himself from being murdered. Regarding this, some say that he deceived the people around him telling them that she was his sister because he was afraid and a coward. But in reality he did not lie to them, but just used his human thought. It is proven by the fact that when he was commanded to leave his country, he had obeyed without fear. So, it is not true that he deceived them telling that she was his sister because he was a coward. He did it, not only because she was really one of his cousins, but also because he thought it better to call her 'sister' rather than 'wife.'

While he was staying in Egypt, Abraham was refined by God so that he might completely rely on God with perfect faith without following human wisdom and thought. He was always ready to obey, but there remained fleshly thoughts in him that were yet to be cast off. Through this trial God allowed for the Pharaoh of Egypt to treat him well. God gave Abraham many blessings including sheep and oxen and donkeys and male and female servants and female donkeys and camels.

This tells us that if trials come upon us because we do not obey we have to suffer difficulties, while if trials come because of fleshly thoughts we have not yet thrown away, even though we are obedient, God causes everything to work for the good.

This trial made it possible for him to say only "Amen" and

obey in everything, and afterwards God commanded him to offer his only son Isaac as a burnt offering. Genesis 22:1 reads, *"Now it came about after these things, that God tested Abraham, and said to him, 'Abraham!' And he said, 'Here I am.'"*

When Isaac was born, Abraham was a hundred years old and his wife, Sarah, was ninety years old. As for the parents it was totally impossible to have a child but only by the grace and promise of God, a son was born to them and the son was counted as more valuable to them than anything else. In addition, he was the seed of the promise of God. That's why he was so amazed when God commanded him to offer his son as a burnt offering like an animal! It was beyond any kind of human imagination.

Because Abraham believed that God would be able to raise his son from death again, however, he could obey the command of God (Hebrews 11:17-19). In other aspect, because all his fleshly thoughts had been destroyed, he could possess the faith in which he could offer his only son Isaac as a burnt offering.

God saw this faith of Abraham and prepared a ram for the burnt offering, so that Abraham might not stretch out his hands against his son. Abraham found a ram caught in the thicket by his horns and took the ram and offered it up for a burnt offering in the place of his son. And he called the name of that place 'The LORD Will Provide.'

God commended Abraham for his faith, saying in Genesis

22:12, *"Now I know that you fear God, since you have not withheld your son, your only son, from Me,"* and gave him amazing promise of blessing in verses 17-18, *"Indeed I will greatly bless you, and I will greatly multiply your seed as the stars of the heavens and as the sand which is on the seashore; and your seed shall possess the gate of their enemies. In your seed all the nations of the earth shall be blessed, because you have obeyed My voice."*

Even if your faith has not reached the level of Abraham's, you may sometimes have experienced the blessing of 'The LORD Will Provide.' When you were about to do something, you found that God had already prepared for it. It was possible because your heart was after God at that moment. If you are able to possess the same faith that Abraham did and completely obey God, you will live in the blessing 'The LORD Will Provide' anywhere and anytime; what an amazing life it is in Christ!

In order for you to receive the blessing of Jehovah-jireh, 'The LORD Will Provide,' you have to say "Amen" to whatever kind of command of God, and walk only according to the will of God without insisting on your own thoughts at all. You have to gain that recognition from God. That's why God clearly tells us that obeying is better than sacrifices (1 Samuel 15:23).

Jesus existed in the form of God, but He did not regard equality with God a thing to be grasped, but He emptied

Himself, took the form of a bond-servant and was made in the likeness of men. And He humbled Himself and became obedient to the point of death (Philippians 2:6-8). And concerning His complete obedience, 2 Corinthians 1:19-20 says, *"For the Son of God, Christ Jesus, who was preached among you by us – by me and Silvanus and Timothy – was not yes and no, but is yes in Him. For as many as are the promises of God, in Him they are yes; therefore also through Him is our Amen to the glory of God through us."*

As the only begotten Son of God said only "Yes," we have to undoubtedly say "Amen" at any word of God and glorify Him by receiving the blessing 'The LORD Will Provide.'

Abraham Pursued Peace and Holiness in Everything

Because he counted the word of God first above all else, and loved Him more than anything else, Abraham said only "Amen" at the word of God and completely obeyed it so that he could please God.

In addition, he became wholly sanctified and always sought to be at peace with everyone around him, so that he could gain recognition from God.

In Genesis 13:8-9, he said to his nephew Lot, *"Please let there be no strife between you and me, nor between my* herdsmen and your herdsmen, for we are brothers. Is not the whole land before you? Please separate from me; if to the left, then I will go to the right; or if to the right, then I will go to the left."

He was senior to Lot, but he gave Lot the choice of the land to make peace and sacrificed himself. It was because he did not seek his own benefits but the other's in his spiritual love. In the same way, if you live in the truth, you should not quarrel nor boast of yourself in order to be at peace with anyone.

In Genesis 14:12, 16, we find that when Abraham heard that his nephew Lot had been taken captive, he set out leading his trained men, born of his house, three hundred and eighteen, and he went in pursuit and brought back all the goods, and also brought back his relative Lot with his possessions, and also the women, and the other people. And because he was completely upright and walked in the right way, he gave Melchizedek, the king of Salem, a tenth of all the gains that were due to Him, and returned the rest of it to the king of Sodom saying *"I will not take a thread or a sandal thong or anything that is yours, for fear you would say, 'I have made Abram rich'"* (v. 23). Thus, Abraham was not only in pursuit of peace in every affair but he also walked in a blameless and upright way.

Hebrews 12:14 says, *"Pursue peace with all men, and the sanctification without which no one will see the Lord."* I eagerly urge you to realize that Abraham could receive the blessing of

Jehovah-jireh, 'The LORD Will Provide,' because he pursued peace with all men and accomplished sanctification. I also urge you to become the same kind of person that he is.

Believing the Power of God the Creator

In order to receive the blessing 'The LORD Will Provide,' we have to believe in the power of God. Hebrews 11:17-19 teach us, *"By faith Abraham, when he was tested, offered up Isaac, and he who had received the promises was offering up his only begotten son it was he to whom it was said, 'In Isaac your descendants shall be called.' He considered that God is able to raise people even from the dead, from which he also received him back as a type."* Abraham believed the power of God the Creator would be able to make everything possible, so he could obey God without following any kind of fleshly and human thoughts.

What would you do if God commands you to offer your only son as a burnt offering? If you believe in the power of God with whom nothing is impossible, no matter how disagreeable it is, you will be able to obey it. Then you will receive the blessing 'The LORD Will Provide.'

As the power of God is limitless, He prepares in advance, accomplishes, and repays us with blessings if we completely obey without having any kind of fleshly thoughts like Abraham.

If we have something we love more than God or say "Amen" only at the things that agree with our thoughts and theories, we can never receive the blessing 'The LORD Will Provide.'

As said in 2 Corinthians 10:5, *"We are destroying speculations and every lofty thing raised up against the knowledge of God, and we are taking every thought captive to the obedience of Christ,"* to receive and experience the blessing 'The LORD Will Provide,' we have to throw away every kind of human thought and posses spiritual faith by which we can say "Amen." Had not Moses possessed spiritual faith, how could he have parted the Red Sea into two? Without spiritual faith, how could Joshua have destroyed the city of Jericho?

If you obey only the things that agree with your own thoughts and knowledge, it cannot be called spiritual obedience. God creates something out of nothingness, so how is His power the same as the strength and knowledge of men who make something out of something?

Matthew 5:39-44 read the following. *"But I say to you, do not resist an evil person; but whoever slaps you on your right cheek, turn the other to him also. If anyone wants to sue you and take your shirt, let him have your coat also. Whoever forces you to go one mile, go with him two. Give to him who asks of you, and do not turn away from him who wants to borrow from you. You have heard that it was said, 'You shall love your neighbor and hate your enemy.' But I say to you, love your enemies and pray for those who persecute you."*

How different is this word of truth of God from our own thoughts and knowledge? That's why I urge you to bear in mind that if you try to say "Amen" only at what is agreeable with your thoughts you cannot accomplish the kingdom of God and receive the blessing Jehovah-jireh, 'The LORD Will Provide.'

Even if you profess the faith in the almighty God, have you been in troubles, anxieties, and worries when faced with any problems? Then, it cannot be considered as true faith. If you have true faith, you have to trust the power of God and commit any problem into His hands with joy and thanksgiving.

May each of you count God as the first, become obedient enough to say only "Amen" to every word of God, pursue peace with all men in holiness, and believe in the power of God who is able to raise the dead again so that you can receive and enjoy the blessing 'The LORD Will Provide,' in the name of our Lord Jesus Christ I pray!

The Author
Dr. Jaerock Lee

Dr. Jaerock Lee was born in Muan, Jeonnam Province, Republic of Korea, in 1943. In his twenties, he suffered from a variety of incurable diseases for seven years and awaited death with no hope for recovery. One day in the spring of 1974, however, he was led to a church by his sister, and when he knelt down to pray, the living God immediately healed him of all his diseases.

From the moment Dr. Lee met the living God through that wonderful experience, he has loved God with all his heart and sincerity, and in 1978 was called to be a servant of God. He prayed fervently so that he could clearly understand the will of God and wholly accomplish it, and obeyed all the word of God. In 1982, he founded Manmin Church in Seoul, S. Korea, and countless works of God, including miraculous healings and wonders, have been taking place at his church.

In 1986, Dr. Lee was ordained as a pastor at the Annual Assembly of Jesus' Sungkyul Church of Korea, and four years later in 1990, his sermons began to be broadcast on the Far East Broadcasting Company, the Asia Broadcast Station, and the Washington Christian Radio System to Australia, Russia, the Philippines, and many more.

Three years later in 1993, Manmin Central Church was selected as one of the "World's Top 50 Churches" by the *Christian World* magazine (US) and he received an Honorary Doctorate of Divinity from Christian Faith College, Florida, USA, and in 1996 a Ph. D. in Ministry from Kingsway Theological Seminary, Iowa, USA.

Since 1993, Dr. Lee has taken the lead in world mission through many overseas crusades in L.A., New York, Baltimore, Hawaii of the USA, Tanzania, Argentina, Uganda, Japan, Pakistan, Kenya, the Philippines, Honduras, India, Russia, Germany, Peru, and Democratic Republic of Congo, and in 2002 he was called a "worldwide pastor" by major Christian newspapers in Korea for his work in various overseas crusades.

As of July 2009, Manmin Central Church is a congregation of more than 100,000 members and has 9,000 branch churches throughout the globe including 52 domestic branch churches in major cities, and has so far commissioned more than 132 missionaries to 25 countries, including the United States, Russia, Germany, Canada, Japan, China, France, India, Kenya, and many more.

To this day, Dr. Lee has written 57 books, including bestsellers *Tasting Eternal Life before Death*, *My Life My Faith I & II*, *The Message of the Cross*, *Heaven I & II*, and *Hell*, and his works have been being translated into more than 40 languages.

Dr. Lee is currently leader of many missionary organizations and associations including: Chairman, The United Holiness Church of Jesus Christ; Permanent President, The World Christianity Revival Mission Association; President, The Nation Evangelization Newspaper; President, Manmin World Mission; Founder, Manmin TV; Founder & Board Chairman, Global Christian Network (GCN); Founder & Board Chairman; World Christian Doctors Network (WCDN); and Founder & Board Chairman, Manmin International Seminary (MIS).

Other powerful books by the same author

Heaven I & II

A detailed sketch of the gorgeous living environment the heavenly citizens enjoy and beautiful description of different levels of heavenly kingdoms.

The Message of the Cross

A powerful awakening message for all the people who are spiritually asleep In this book you will find the reason Jesus is the only Savior and the true love of God.

Hell

An earnest message to all mankind from God, who wishes not even one soul to fall into the depths of hell! You will discover the never-before-revealed account of the cruel reality of the Lower Grave and hell.

Tasting Eternal Life Before Death

A testimonial memoirs of Dr. Jaerock Lee, who was born gain and saved from the valley of death and has been leading an exemplary Christian life.

The Measure of Faith

What kind of a dwelling place, crown and reward are prepared for you in heaven? This book provides with wisdom and guidance for you to measure your faith and cultivate the best and most mature faith.

www.urimbooks.com

www.ingramcontent.com/pod-product-compliance
Lightning Source LLC
LaVergne TN
LVHW021226080526
838199LV00089B/5838